Kirkbymoorside, Rosedale and Farndale

by
Malcolm Boyes and Hazel Chester

Dalesman

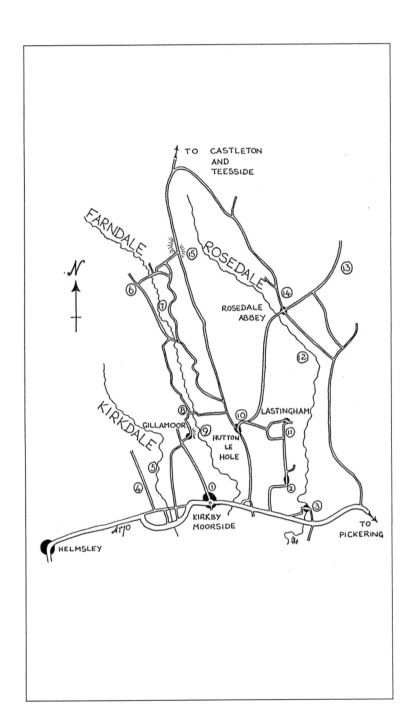

Contents

Introduction 4

Walk 1   Kirkbymoorside's Castles 6

Walk 2   Appleton Common 9

Walk 3   Sinnington Circuit 12

Walk 4   The Woods of Kirkdale 15

Walk 5   Robin Hood's Howl 18

Walk 6   Rudland Rigg and a Corpse Road 21

Walk 7   The Daffodils of Farndale 24

Walk 8   Lowna and the River Dove 27

Walk 9   Gillamoor Mill and Lowna 30

Walk 10   Hutton le Hole and Lastingham 33

Walk 11   Gallows Hill and Spaunton 35

Walk 12   Hollins Mine, Rosedale 38

Walk 13   Hamer Moor 41

Walk 14   The Hidden Dale 44

Walk 15   The Rosedale Railway 46

THE DALESMAN PUBLISHING COMPANY LTD,
CLAPHAM, via Lancaster, LA2 8EB

First published 1992

© MALCOLM BOYES AND HAZEL CHESTER

ISBN: 1 85568 042 4

Typeset by Lands Services, East Molesey, Surrey
Printed by Peter Fretwell & Sons Ltd., Keighley, West Yorkshire BD21 1PZ

INTRODUCTION

Kirkbymoorside lies below the southern edge of the North York Moors National Park and makes an excellent base for touring the area. Most of the walks are set within the National Park. The scenic moorland road from Castleton provides a link into this area for motorists and walkers from Cleveland. All the walks are circular and no other transport is required.

The walks range between 2½ and 6½ miles and provide an afternoon's stroll for all the family. If you are more ambitious a walk can be undertaken in the morning, then after a break at an inn, or for a picnic, a further walk in the afternoon. These are walks to be enjoyed so take a field guide to birds and flowers and a pair of binoculars. See how many plants you can identify – but don't pick them, leave them to give pleasure to someone else. An early morning or late evening walk may offer a richer variety of bird and animal life. The selected routes pass through a wide variety of landscapes including farmland, deciduous woodland, forestry, moorland and rough pasture each supporting a range of birds and plants.

Fine clear days at any time of the year are most suitable for the walks. In August and September the moors form a purple carpet as the heather blooms. In April the wild daffodils in Farndale are usually at their best and four of the walks visit the areas best known for seeing the flowers in bloom. In early spring the hedges and trees are beginning to bud and leaf after the winter. Equally the autumn offers its own spectacular display as the leaves turn brown. A fine day in winter with a hint of snow on the tops can provide some of the finest views over the countryside as you walk along frozen tracks.

The walks have been selected for interest, visiting churches, former mills, a mineral railway or an ironstone mine. Some were selected for their woodland paths and all pass through areas of scenic interest. If you are on holiday in the area and encounter a wet day you can visit Kirkdale or Lastingham churches, the Ryedale Folk Museum at Hutton le Hole or the nearby Beck Isle Museum at Pickering. Further information can be found in the two Dalesman books Exploring the North York Moors and Exploring York's Countryside.

Equipment
ON a dry summer afternoon all the walks can be accomplished in sensible walking shoes. After rain some tracks may become muddy and boots may be preferred. You will require a windproof jacket

as moorland breezes can soon make you cold and uncomfortable. With the uncertainties of the British weather it may be worth taking some waterproof clothing. You may wish to take a compass and the relevant Ordnance Survey map is Sheet 94 in the 1:50000 series; all the walks are on Sheet 100 except for part of Walk 15. The area is also covered by the Ordnance Survey tourist map. In the Ordnance Survey 1:25000 series you require both the North York Moors east and west sheets to cover all the walks in the book. If you wish to take binoculars and a camera the easiest way to carry these is in a small rucksack.

Safety

IF you have an accident or meet someone else who has had an accident render what first aid is possible and the local rescue team can be contacted by ringing the police. Don't let members of your group stray out of sight or get left behind. If the moor tops are covered, or likely to become covered in mist, choose a walk in the dale bottom. The moorland walks with their extensive views are best attempted on clear days.

Problems with paths

THE walk descriptions are correct at the time of writing. Some paths may become overgrown and some may be diverted but the new route will be well signposted. With modern farming methods hedges or stiles may disappear or new buildings appear around farms, however the path should still remain walkable. In case of difficulty contact the Highways Department at County Hall, Northallerton.

Parking

EACH of the walks starts from a point where you can park your car, either in a village, in a car park or on a piece of land where cars park regularly. Please do not obstruct other traffic or farm gateways. A grid reference is given to pinpoint the start. Details for calculating a grid reference are given on Ordnance Survey maps.

Warning 1

THIEVES operate around the car parks in the area. Do not leave cameras, purses, handbags or other valuables on view in your car. Take them with you or lock them in the boot.

Warning 2

PLEASE drive carefully on unfenced moorland roads and give sheep and lambs the right of way.

Kirkbymoorside's Castles

Parking: (SE697861) The car park near the roundabout on the A170 in Kirkbymoorside.

VERY little remains of Kirkbymoorside's two castles but it was because of the castles, the weekly market and the annual fair granted by the castle's owners that the place grew into a small town. The first castle to the east of the town on Vivers Hill was built in the middle of the 12th century. From the site you can look down on the town. By the late 14th century this castle had decayed. By the early 15th century the estate had passed through marriage to the Neville Family who built a new castle to the north of the town. The castle had corner towers linked by walls of which a small portion remains today.

Start:
FROM the car park walk up the road into Kirkbymoorside. On the right you pass the unusual building with a cast iron façade inscribed 'C. Carter Gas Works'. At the roundabout near the White Horse fork right and walk up Church Street. Fork left passing a stone mounting block on your right. Continue for fifty yards then turn left at a sign towards the church, climb some steps to a gate into the churchyard and turn right. Keep the beech hedge on your left as you cross the churchyard and in fifty yards turn right to a kissing gate. Continue up the field to cross a stile. Turn left and follow the edge of the field round to a seat. This high ground was the site of Kirkbymoorside's first castle.

Return the way you came to the kissing gate into the churchyard and turn right keeping the churchyard wall on your left. Pass through a kissing gate and walk diagonally over the field to a gate onto a side road. Turn left for thirty yards, then turn right up Castlegate. When the road sweeps left carry straight on to two stiles. Keep the fence on your left as you leave Kirkbymoorside behind and begin walking north over the fields. After three fields you reach a reservoir, turn right for twenty yards then turn left over a stile. Follow the edge of the field to cross two more stiles close together and after a further two fields turn left along a broad farm track.

Bear left at High Park Farm through a white metal gate and continue with the hedge and fence on your right. At the end of the field turn left keeping the hedge and golf course on your right. Pass through a gate and continue straight ahead on the track along

KIRKBYMOORSIDE'S CASTLES
WALK No 1

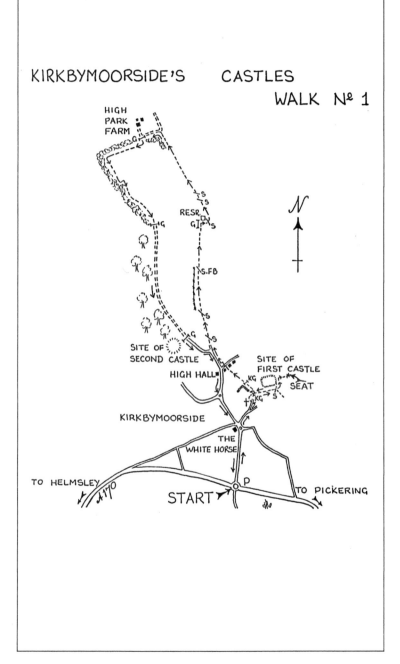

the top edge of a wooded valley. As you approach the outskirts of Kirkbymoorside you reach the site of the town's second castle. Pass through the gateway and between the new houses built on the site of the castle. Follow the road to the right and descend. Fork right and pass High Hall set back from the road on your right. At the mini roundabout fork left into the town centre and continue straight ahead back to the car park.

Appleton Common

Parking: (SE735878) Street parking in Appleton le Moors.

THE village of Appleton le Moors consists of one broad main street flanked by attractive stone houses. One of the houses carries three carved faces on the front façade and another carries a fire mark dating back to the time when insurance companies would bear the cost of saving a burning building.

The church was built in 1865 for Mrs Shepherd as a memorial to her husband Joseph Shepherd. At the end of the village stands a rough stone marker known as Low Cross which is one of 13 stone crosses passed by walkers completing the annual North York Moors Crosses Walk in July. High Cross, a broken stone shaft in a high socket stone stands 400 yards further north and in the Middle Ages travellers could have sighted through the hole in Low Cross to High Cross to find the direction to travel to Ana Cross 3½ miles away on the moorland skyline. Before the coming of signposts wayside crosses acted as markers to guide travellers over the featureless moors.

Start:
WALK up the main street past the church to the road junction where you can see Low Cross on the grass to the right of the junction. Return to the church and turn right along the lane opposite. Pass a children's playground in a field on your right and continue along the broad lane. It may be worth your while to walk quietly to see what birds there are in the hedges on either side.

At the end of the lane turn left, ignore the public footpath and bridleway signs. The broad farm lane leads down to the edge of Appleton Common. In front of you at the end of the lane is a seat and stone pillar set among fourteen trees, a memorial to Catherine McDougall who lived from 1890 to 1950. Turn left beside the road with the open common on your right which is grazed by sheep.

After 700 yards turn right at a public footpath sign. Ignore the road to the sewage treatment works and take the grassy path keeping the valley on your left. At a fork in the track bear right and continue through the bushes and nearby gorse until you see a metal gate ahead. Fifty yards before the gate bear right on a track that skirts the fields keeping the fence on your left. This area of open common could yield a number of interesting birds including the colourful stonechat. Continue through the bushes on the

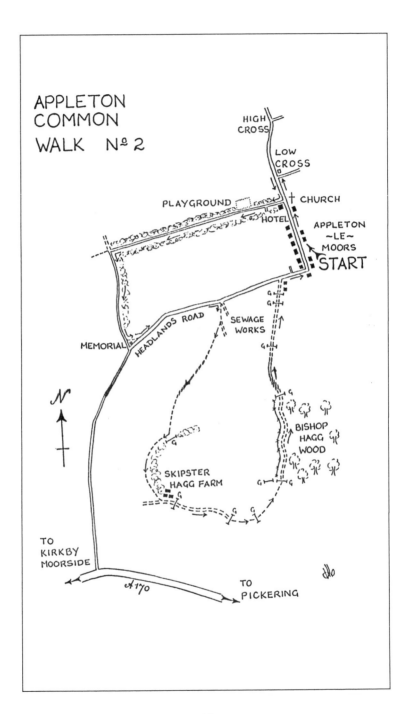

APPLETON
COMMON
WALK Nº 2

HIGH CROSS

LOW CROSS

PLAYGROUND

† CHURCH

HOTEL

APPLETON
~LE~
MOORS

START

MEMORIAL

HEADLANDS ROAD

SEWAGE WORKS

N

BISHOP
HAGG
WOOD

SKIPSTER
HAGG FARM

TO
KIRKBY
MOORSIDE

A170

TO
PICKERING

common with the fields on your left until you reach the road to Skipster Hagg Farm.

Turn left along the farm road and pass in front of the farm. Continue through a metal gate and along a grassy stoned track over the field, it eventually swings right to a gate in a small valley. Continue up the other side of the valley and pass through a gate. Bear left across the field to the right hand one of a pair of gates. The broad path now has a fence on your left. The path passes the side of Bishop Hagg Wood and continues through gates over The Riggs to join the road on the outskirts of Appleton le Moors. Turn right, the house on the corner when the road swings left into the village carries a Yorkshire Insurance Company fire mark above the front door. Walk back up the main street to where you started.

Sinnington Circuit

Parking: (SE743857) Street parking in Sinnington.

THE village of Sinnington lies to the north of the Kirkbymoorside-to-Pickering road. Many of the stone houses stand around the spacious green with a tiny stone bridge which once was used to cross a mill stream. The small village church dates back to Saxon times but was restored in 1904. There are several ancient stones built into the walls which have served other purposes, for example there is part of a Saxon cross showing the crucifixion and another piece of a cross showing knotwork.

Close to the church the walk passes the oldest medieval building still standing in the area, apart from churches and castles. In the 12th century it was the Great Hall of the Barons de Clere who came from Rouen in France. On the eastern side of the hall there is a 12th century window; the other windows date from the 15th century.

The walk passes through Cropton Bank Wood which provides a good opportunity to see birds and grey squirrels, probably the best time being in the morning. It would be worth keeping an eye open for nuthatch, treecreeper and chiff chaff as well as the more usual woodland birds.

The walk descends to the River Seven at Nutholm. The present building carries a date of 1818 but an earlier house was the birth-place, on May 3rd 1760, of William Scoresby. Eventually he became the most successful whaling captain of his time sailing out of Whitby. In those days whale oil was the main source of lighting in homes and whale bones had many uses from corsets to bed bases. Probably he would remember the boyhood summers he had spent around the Seven Valley as long voyages to the Arctic took place during the summer returning home for the winter months.

Start:
FROM the road bridge in the centre of the village, facing upstream, turn left away from the village green. There is a foot-path beside the road and the river is on your left. Pass Friars Hill Farm and turn left at the public footpath sign, cross the edge of the field keeping the farm buildings on your left. A long stile in the corner of the field crosses a gutter. Pass through a metal gate and cross diagonally over the field to a stile. Follow the path beside this pleasant section to a footbridge where you cross the river.

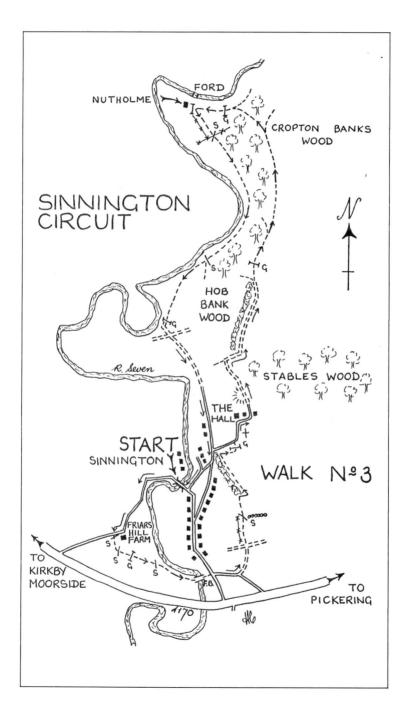

SINNINGTON CIRCUIT

FORD
NUTHOLME
CROPTON BANKS WOOD

N

HOB BANK WOOD

R. Seven

STABLES WOOD

THE HALL

START
SINNINGTON

WALK Nº 3

FRIARS HILL FARM

TO KIRKBY MOORSIDE

TO PICKERING

A170

Walk along the side road opposite the bridge and after 100 yards turn left along a broad stone track. Cross over a farm track and continue along the side of the field with a wire fence on your left. Cross a stile set in a stone wall and a small stone flag bridge and continue to the end of the field where you turn right for 50 yards then turn left and follow the edge of the next field to a gate at the top near the church. On reaching the road turn right, then left at the church. In front of you is the medieval, stone built Great Hall among the farm buildings. Turn right in front of the hall and follow the concrete road round to the left, then continue straight ahead along the broad track.

As you climb past the edge of Stables Wood look back to the left into the village of Sinnington. From this point there is an extensive view over the surrounding countryside. At the end of the next field follow the indicated bridleway to the right, then turn left at the next sign on a path beside a hedge and fence. After 150 yards turn right onto a path that leads to a gate in a wood. Continue along the path on the top edge of the woodland for one mile, then take the broad track which forks left and descends through mixed woodland.

Pass through a gate into a field and continue towards the cottage of Nutholme. Turn left just before the next gate, along the wire fence, keeping it on your right. The path returns back through the woodland with the river on your right. At the end of the wood cross a stile into a field and fork right towards the river. When the river swings right continue ahead to a gate which leads to a broad track. The track climbs, crosses over another track and continues back into Sinnington where you cross over the green back to the bridge.

The Woods of Kirkdale

Parking: (SE668859) There are wide grass verges in Hold Caldron Lane. Drive west from Kirkbymoorside on the A170 for 1½ miles. Turn right at the signpost to Kirkdale ½ mile, turn left at the T junction then take the first turn right, signposted Skiplam only. Hold Caldron Lane is the first turning right after Lund Court Farm.

THIS route offers a fine woodland walk through the quiet valley of Kirkdale. The valley bottom has a series of grass fields fringed by deciduous trees while the loftier valley sides are covered in conifers. The walk passes three interesting buildings. Kirkdale Minster, which is detailed in Walk 5. Hold Caldron Mill, where the inhabitants of Fadmoor had their corn ground, has obscure origins but a stone was once sited on the building inscribed with the date of 1784 and the name Peter Peat. William Baldwin was the miller in 1840. After climbing out of the valley the walk passes Skiplam Grange. It became a grange of Rievaulx Abbey in the middle of the 12th century and the last abbot of Rievaulx used to come here each summer to hunt, a right given to the grange by Henry III.

Start:
WALK down Hold Caldron Lane and when the road begins to descend turn right through a gate signposted public bridleway. To the left is an excellent view into Kirkdale where you will be walking later. Follow the path along the valley top, after 100 yards fork right to a gate and continue along the edge of the field with the wood on your left. After 700 yards turn left through a white gate and descend to a road junction. Turn left down the road to the interesting Kirkdale Minster standing beside Hodge Beck in its remote setting.

After visiting the church continue to a hunting gate and into a field. Keep the fence and wood on your left. Cross a small bridge over the river and follow the track over the field and into a wood with the stream on your left below. At the junction of tracks go straight ahead into the trees and in 15 yards fork left under beech trees. At the end of the field the path becomes a broad track which continues to Hold Caldron Mill. As you approach the mill cross a stile and pass the mill on your left. After 70 yards fork left and cross a stile beside a gate. Follow the track over the field eventually skirting the edge of a wood on your right to reach a gate.

Continue along the track and after ¼ mile fork right over a stile

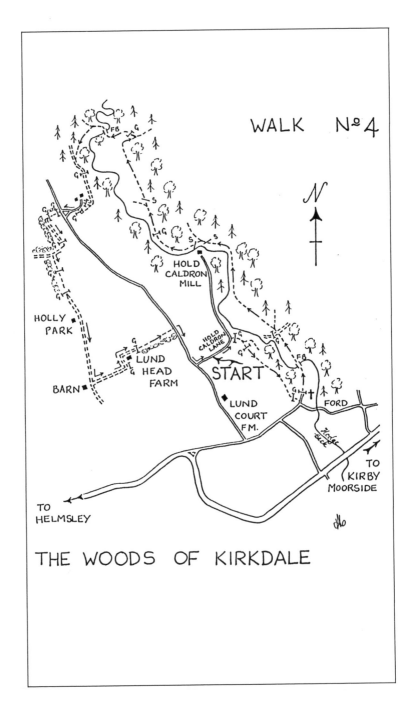

WALK N⁰ 4

N

HOLD
CALDRON
MILL

HOLLY
PARK

LUND
HEAD
FARM

HOLD
CALDRON
LANE

START

FB

FORD

BARN

LUND
COURT
F.M.

TO
KIRBY
MOORSIDE

TO
HELMSLEY

THE WOODS OF KIRKDALE

16

opposite a belt of hawthorn trees and continue through the wood. After 600 yards turn back left through a gate marked with a sign of a man with a rucksack. Keep the old hedge on your right as you approach the river then continue to a footbridge. At the other side of Hodge Beck bear left and follow the track up the hillside. At the top of the first climb fork left and in 200 yards you join a forestry road. Continue climbing and the track eventually leads to Skiplam Grange. As you approach the farm bear left across a field to a gate into the access road. Turn left then fork right to the road.

Pass through the gate opposite and cross the field keeping the hedge on your left, pass through a gate and turn left along Guneroft Lane. Pass through a gate at the end of the lane and turn right. At the end of the field turn left and follow the hedge on your right down past Holly Park Farm. Continue down the tarmac road and turn left opposite a barn along the access road to Lund Head Farm. At the farm the access lane turns left then right around the buildings and continues over the fields to a road. Turn right and Hold Caldron Lane is the first turning left.

Robin Hood's Howl

Parking: (SE684854) About a mile west of Kirkbymoorside is a roadside car park. The car park at Kirkdale Church is for people visiting the church only.

A howl, which forms part of the name of this walk, is a local name for a wooded valley. The route passes the site of Kirkdale Cave. When the hillside was being quarried in the 1820's the bones of tigers, bears, bisons and elephants were discovered in a cave. They were believed to have been taken into the cave by hyenas 70,000 years ago.

Kirkdale Church dates from Saxon times and stands alone in this quiet peaceful valley where it serves a number of nearby villages and hamlets. Above the south doorway is a Saxon sundial recording the churches rebuilding by Orm in the time of Edward the Confessor 1042–1066. The remoteness of the churchyard led to illicit burials of Roman Catholics in 1611.

Start:
FROM the car park walk along the road to Helmsley, then turn right along the road signposted Fadmoor 2½. Turn left at the crossroads on the road signposted Kirkdale ¼. The road descends into a wooded valley, on your right is a quarry where Kirkdale Cave was situated. Bear right and cross a footbridge over Hodge Beck when the road crosses a ford. Continue up the road to the junction and turn right down to St. Gregory's Minster. Pass the car park with a stone mounting block and bear left on the track beside the churchyard wall, though don't forget to visit this interesting church.

The path beside the churchyard leads to a hunting gate and into a field. Keeping the fence and wood on your left the path leads to a small bridge over the river. Follow the broad track over the field and into a wood with the stream below you on your left. At the junction of tracks go straight ahead into the trees and in 15 yards fork right up a path through mixed woodland. Keep your eyes open for birds. At the top turn right, away from a gate and descend back down into the valley on a broad track. At the junction in the valley bottom turn left up the valley.

Just before you reach a gate which leads into farmland turn sharp left between hedges on a waymarked path. A short climb leads to a hunting gate, turn right keeping the hedge on your right.

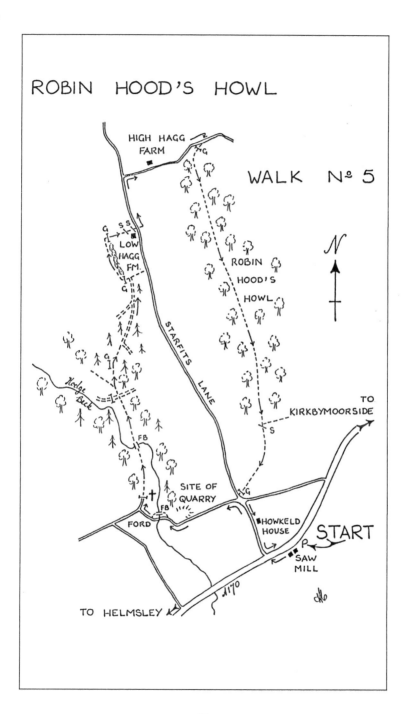

ROBIN HOOD'S HOWL

WALK N° 5

HIGH HAGG FARM

ROBIN HOOD'S HOWL

LOW HAGG FM.

STARFITS LANE

Hodge Beck

FB

SITE OF QUARRY

FORD

HOWKELD HOUSE

START

SAW MILL

TO KIRKBYMOORSIDE

TO HELMSLEY

19

At the end of the field turn right through a gate and and follow the track towards Low Hagg Farm. Turn left over a stile before the farm buildings and cross the field used as a caravan site to another stile onto the road.

Turn left up the road and turn right at the first road junction to pass High Hagg Farm. The road descends into a wooded valley. As you climb out of the valley turn right through a wooden gate at a public footpath sign. The track follows the wooded valley bottom which is called Robin Hood's Howl. Again there is an opportunity to see a variety of woodland birds. At the end of the wood cross over a stile and continue straight ahead along the shallow valley. Eventually you have a fence on your right which leads to a gate back to a crossroads. Take the road opposite signposted Welburn ¾ and turn right at the main road to the car park.

Rudland Rigg and a Corpse Road

Parking: (SE672952) Low Mill car park, Farndale. When the daffodils are in season an extra field is open for a small charge. At this time a one way system operates in the dale.

THE walk passes through the remote side valley of West Gill, off Farndale, the climb onto the heather clad moors reveals excellent views. The hillside was mined in the 19th century for hard jet to supply the jet jewellery manufacturers in Whitby. The jet was usually found along a line about 900 feet above sea level but all that remains today of the industry is a few shale heaps. Along the ridge top is the ancient road called Rudland Rigg. It was used by travellers passing between Kirkbymoorside and Stokesley and may have been in use for 2,000 years.

The descent back into Farndale is down Monket Bank this route westwards into Bransdale was used as a corpse road. Anyone dying in Upper Farndale was carried over the ridge to Cockayne Church in Bransdale which obtained burial rights in 1665. The route returns along the daffodil walk beside the River Dove.

Start:
FROM the car park turn right along the road for ¼ of a mile. Beware of traffic as the road is narrow. Turn left over a cattle grid at a bridleway to Rudland Rigg sign. Walk up the farm access road, you can see the remains of an old paved footpath in places. In front there is a good view of Horn Ridge and Horn End Crag which separate West Gill from Farndale. Cross over a cattle grid at Horn End Farm and carry straight ahead when the track bears right to Horn End Cottages. The grassy track bends right, then left, then right again to a gate. Continue along the edge of the fields eventually keeping High Barn on your left.

Fifty yards beyond High Barn bear left at two gateposts, where a bridleway sign indicates the route. Continue with the wall on your right to a gate. Cross the footbridge over West Gill Beck and a stile into a field. Climb the slope to a gateway in the wall on your left. Follow the sunken track up the hillside which bears left then swings right to a gateway. There are excellent views back into Farndale and into this side valley of West Gill.

Continue along the gently rising path which climbs the hillside to Rudland Rigg on the moor top. Bracken can be a nuisance in summer but the superb views compensate. As you climb you pass

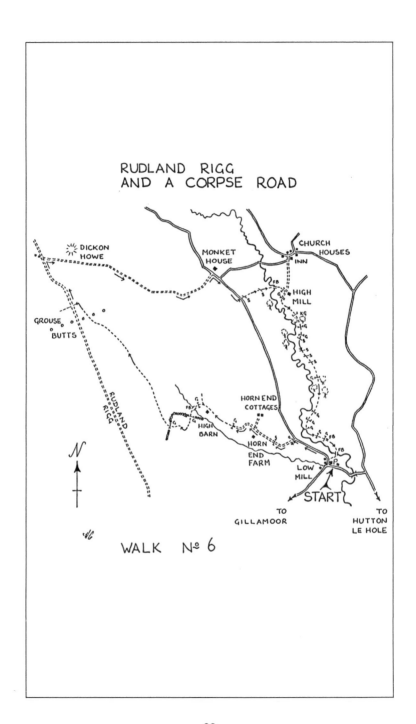

RUDLAND RIGG
AND A CORPSE ROAD

WALK Nº 6

through the area where the jet was mined. As you pass a line of grouse butts you can start looking left for the broad moorland road that has never been surfaced. When you reach the road bear right. The track you have just climbed was used as a short cut by travellers wanting to be into the southern part of Farndale until a landslip swept away part of the route.

Continue along Rudland Rigg for half a mile and turn right at a crossroads of tracks. Follow the broad track over the moor passing Dicken Howe on your left. This was the track used by traffic passing between Farndale and Bransdale including coffins carrying the dead for burial in Cockayne Church. Eventually the track begins to fall away more steeply and an excellent view opens out into Upper Farndale. This area was the part of the dale the water authorities wanted to flood and turn into a reservoir for Hull.

The broad track descends steeply into Farndale joining a tarmac road at Monket House. Turn right passing straight over a road junction and after 150 yards turn left over a stile signposted 'public path to Church Houses'. Descend along the edge of the field crossing another stile to reach a footbridge over the River Dove. At the far side turn right over the field to a gate. Turn right along the track and pass between the buildings of High Mill.

Continue through the gate and cross the field to two stone posts. Follow the distinct path south with the River Dove on your right. This is part of the famous daffodil walk between Church Houses and Low Mill which now forms part of the Farndale Nature Reserve. After a mile you reach a footbridge where you turn right along a path that leads to the road where you turn left back into the car park.

The Daffodils of Farndale

Parking: (SE672952) Low Mill car park, Farndale. When the daffodils are in season an extra field is open for a small charge. At this time a one way system operates in the dale.

THE walk beside the River Dove between Low Mill and Church Houses is the most popular walk for visitors wishing to see the wild daffodils each year. Wild daffodils can also be seen on Walk 6 and around Lowna on Walks 8 and 9. There are three alternatives to this walk, the return can be made from Church Houses back along the riverside which would be 3¼ miles in length or you can turn right before High Mill to Bragg Farm and follow a route over the fields giving a wider view of Farndale. The full route gives a little road walking but passes the Feversham Arms Inn at Church Houses and also the church. There is usually a fine display of daffodils in the churchyard during the season. Out of the daffodil season Farndale reverts to a quiet valley with only a few cars on the twisty roads but the peace and solitude in summer add to the walks appeal. The area is a nature reserve and the flowers should not be picked or damaged.

Start:
WALK to the corner of the car park near the road and turn right on the path signposted to High Mill. Cross over a footbridge over the River Dove and turn left following the distinct path. As you continue with the river on your left pass over a number of gates and stiles. After a mile of walking you come out of the lightly wooded path through a kissing gate into a field; there is another gate twenty yards to the right on another path that leads back to High Wold House. At this point you have to decide if you want to walk the short route.

The short walk leaves the riverside path 30 yards into the field. Turn right climbing to a new gate beside a tree. Then keep the fence on your right to a gate; continue climbing with the hedge on your left towards the farm. Turn left, then right through a gate and continue. Pass through a gate, bear left through another gate and pass to the left of the farm buildings. At a signpost on the field corner turn right to a gate above Bragg Farm and continue ahead on the track. The return to the car park is described after the next two paragraphs.

The longer walk continues over the fields to High Mill. As you

THE DAFFODILS OF FARNDALE

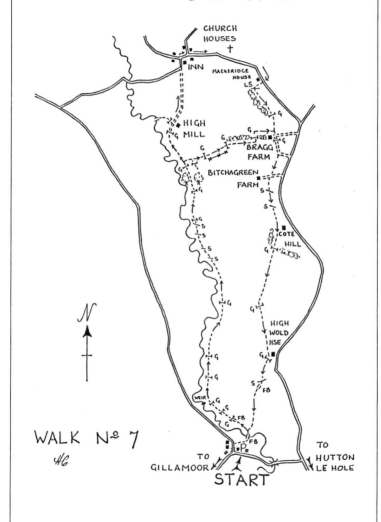

CHURCH
HOUSES
†

INN

MACKERIDGE
HOUSE
LS

HIGH
MILL

BRAGG
FARM

BITCHAGREEN
FARM

COTE
HILL

HIGH
WOLD
HSE

WEIR

FB

FB

FB

N

WALK Nº 7

TO
GILLAMOOR
START

P

TO
HUTTON
LE HOLE

approach the mill buildings you pass two large gateposts. The one on the left bears the letters I.G.; I.W.F.; J.S.; 1826. The first letters could refer to Isaac Garbutt who was a farmer at Church Houses in 1840. The first building on the right was a blacksmith's shop. The next building was the mill, powered by water from Blakey Gill. The water passed through a wooden launder at the back of the building and onto the overshot wheel. The track between the buildings leads into Church Houses meeting the road near the Feversham Arms Inn. You can return back along the same route to view the daffodils from a different angle; this walk would be 3¼ miles long.

To continue on the walk and see more of Farndale turn right along the road beyond the inn. When you reach the junction fork right along the road to Hutton le Hole. Pass the church on your left and climb to pass Mackeridge House on your right. Beyond the house turn right on the signposted footpath. Keep the wall on your left to a ladder stile over the wall, then keep the hedge on your right and pass through a gate. Pass above Bragg Farm where the short route joins the longer route.

From Bragg Farm pass through a gateway and continue along a track. After 200 yards the path crosses the field to Bitchagreen Farm. Cross the stone wall and keep the farm on your right. Cross the field to a stile and pass below a cottage, then cross another stile towards Cote Hill. Keep the new barn on the left and drop down to the right hand field gate. Follow the broad track eventually bearing left at the end of the field. Walk along a track to High Wold House. In the farmyard turn right through a gate and descend gradually to a stile and footbridge over the stream. A track which is partly paved leads down to the River Dove near the footbridge you crossed near the start. Climb back to the car park at Low Mill.

Lowna and The River Dove

Parking: (SE685910) Lowna car park. From Hutton le Hole take the road north to Castleton. Take the first turn left to Gillamoor. After a mile cross a bridge and in 200 yards turn right into a small car park.

LOWNA Mill was a fulling mill in the 17th and 18th centuries (see walk 9). Later the mill became a tannery. Copious supplies of water were required for tanning hide. This was run off from the river and diverted along water channels to various steeping pits inside the mill, here the hides were steeped in solutions of varying strength of water and tree bark. When the tanning was completed the hides were dried in sheds with louvred doors to allow a movement of air. These can still be seen.

The walk passes the Society of Friends burial ground at Lowna. After Sarkless Kitty was drowned (see walk 9) her body disappeared. The local community was deciding if she had committed suicide, if so, she couldn't be buried in the churchyard. It is now believed that a local couple who had lost a daughter of about the same age buried Sarkless Kitty's body with their daughter in the new grave in the burial ground.

Start:
FROM the end of the car park follow the track that eventually descends to a footbridge. Follow the track to the right, then fork left along the path signposted 'Low Mill via Park Farm'. After 200 yards you pass the dry stone wall enclosure of Lowna burial ground on your left. Continue along the hollow way with a wall on your right to a gate which leads to a broad track, this climbs gently through the forestry.

When you leave the wood continue ahead on the track until you reach a farm road. There are some pleasant views to the right as you cross over the moor. At the farm road turn right over the moor to a stile beside a gate. The right of way should go straight down the hillside but it has been planted with young trees. The easiest way is to follow the broad track which passes through the gate, it takes an easier gradient down the hill then turns back right to another stile beside a gate.

Follow the wire fence on your right and eventually it swings left and descends to a footbridge over the River Dove. Bear left up a track between stone walls. When you reach the stream turn back

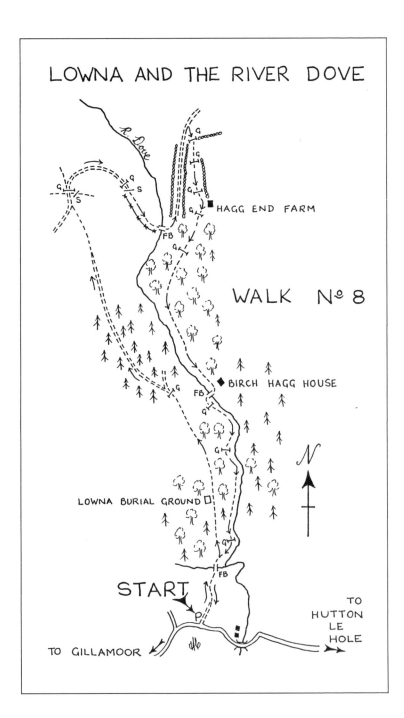

LOWNA AND THE RIVER DOVE

WALK Nº 8

R. Dove

HAGG END FARM

FB

BIRCH HAGG HOUSE

N

LOWNA BURIAL GROUND

FB

START

P

TO GILLAMOOR

TO HUTTON LE HOLE

right through a gateway in a stone wall. Cross the field to a gate then keep the wall on your left to pass below Hagg End Farm. The farm carries a stone carved with D.J. 1897. This may commemorate Queen Victoria's Diamond Jubilee in 1897. The track continues along the edge of the field to a gate. Cross the next field to a gate that leads to a delightful woodland path.

The path leads down towards the river and passes in front of Birch Hagg House. Turn right over the footbridge and left through a gate. The riverside path you now follow has one of the finest displays of wild daffodils when they are in season. Keep the riverside on your left until you swing right to the footbridge you crossed near the start. Turn left over the bridge and climb back to the car park.

Walk 9   **Distance 5 miles**

Gillamoor Mill and Lowna

Parking: (SE705903) Hutton le Hole car park.

IF you approach or return from this walk via the Surprise View at
Gillamoor you can look down on the greater part of this walk.
Gillamoor Mill may date back to Saxon times and it is mentioned
in records of the 12th century. A date stone on the building is
inscribed 'I.E.S. 1779' and probably records a rebuilding.

Near the mill is a ford associated with the ghost of Sarkless Kitty.
She was a local girl who drowned in the river. Her ghost appeared
without a sark or petticoat, i.e. naked, to passers by. A number of
people were drowned at the ford over the following years until the
place was exorcised with bell, book and candle. Kitty may be buried
in Lowna burial ground (see Walk 8).

Near the bridge at Lowna is a farm and former mill. It probably
dates back to the 13th century and was used as a fulling mill.
Fulling mills pounded the new woollen cloth to remove grease and
force the wool strands into stronger cloth. The walk above Lowna
provides an excellent display of wild daffodils in the season.

Start:
FROM the car park turn left towards Hutton le Hole and turn
right at the junction signposted to Castleton. Walk up the road
noting the pleasant scene on the right as Hutton Beck tumbles
over a small waterfall. At the second junction turn left towards
Gillamoor and after 50 yards fork left at a public footpath sign passing a sign saying 'Barmoor access only'. Fork right on a grassy
track in front of Barmoor Lodge and continue with the wall on
your left. Carry straight on along a moorland track when the stone
wall ends.

Eventually the path bears to the right of a field. When you see a
footbridge on your right continue to a gate and track and turn back
right, then turn left over the footbridge. Cross the field to a stile
near a tree below the farm, cross the next field to a stile in the field
corner. Turn left and continue with the hedge on your left to cross
a stile and continue over a footbridge to the mill. Cross over the
mill leet and pass the building on your left.

Turn left through a white metal gate, then turn right along the
access road until you reach the tarmac road. Turn right downhill
and at the road junction fork right. In 100 yards turn left through
the signposted car park, and continue along the track descending

30

GILLAMOOR MILL AND LOWNA

WALK N° 9

to a footbridge. Bear right on the track to a fork and turn right on the track signposted 'To Low Mill via Hagg End'. Keep the stream on your right to a gate, then continue with the river on your right. These fields provide a fine display of wild daffodils in the season. Eventually you pass to the right of a barn and turn right over a wooden bridge. Turn right along the broad track, it passes through the deciduous wood with the river on your right until you reach the road. Turn left up the unfenced moorland road. After a mile you reach the Castleton-to-Hutton le Hole road. Turn right into Hutton le Hole and left to reach the car park.

Hutton le Hole and Lastingham

Parking: (SE705903) Hutton le Hole car park.

TWO picturesque villages nestle in hollows between the Tabular Hills and the southern edge of the moors. Hutton le Hole is linked by a narrow strip of farmland to Lastingham. On this walk you can look south over the fields to the wooded slopes of the Tabular Hills while the moorland climbs away to the north. Both villages have places of interest. Close to the stream in the centre of Lastingham is St. Cedd's Well. St. Cedd built a monastery here in 654 at the request of King Ethelwald. It was destroyed in the 9th century by raiding Danes but rebuilt by Benedictine monks in 1078. Inside the present day church you can descend into the crypt that dates from that time.

On the return through Hutton le Hole the walk passes the well known Ryedale Folk Museum. There are a number of houses, barns and other buildings rebuilt on the site and furnished with contemporary furnishings and equipment. This gives an interesting look at the surrounding area in earlier times. An annual merrils contest is held each September in the manor house in the museum, this is a board game that has been played in the area for centuries.

Start:
FROM the large car park cross over the road opposite the toilets to a stone enclosure. This was the pinfold where stray animals were impounded by the pinder, they were returned to their owner on payment of a small fine. Turn right and follow the road which sweeps right and crosses the unfenced moorland edge towards Lastingham. After half a mile the road crosses over Fairy Call Beck. In local folk lore you had to be careful crossing the stream at night or the fairies would blow out your lantern light.

At the top of the short climb after the bridge take note of the signposted public footpath sign on your right as this is the way you will return. Continue along the road for half a mile then turn left fifty yards before the second bridge at the public footpath sign. The track leads to a stile and continues, swinging right, on the moorland side of the fields. When the field edge leads to Camomile Farm bear left to the field corner and continue ahead. The path descends steeply to Hole Beck which can be crossed on stepping stones. A steep climb then leads to a seat, there is a glorious view of the wood topped heights to the south and back to Hutton le Hole.

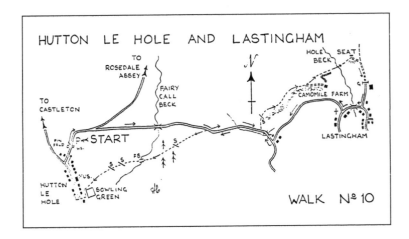

Continue bearing right and descend to a gate which leads to a road into Lastingham. At the junction turn right and descend to the bridge with St. Cedd's Well on the right. Continue to the road junction and church. Turn right past the inn and walk back along the road. Turn right at the next road junction over the bridge and past the path you used earlier. Continue beside the moorland road to the signposted footpath above Fairy Call Beck.

Fork left at the public footpath sign along a grassy track which leads through the wood to a footbridge. Then keep the fence on your right to a stile. Over to the right you can see some of the buildings forming the Ryedale Folk Museum. Cross the field to another stile and continue passing to the right of the bowling green as you approach the village. Turn left at the stone wall, pass through a gate and follow the track to the road in the village. Turn right passing the entrance to the Ryedale Folk Museum which also has free entrance to its interesting shop. Continue, turning right back to the car park.

Gallows Hill and Spaunton

Parking: (SE728904) Street parking in Lastingham.

THE picturesque village of Lastingham nestles under the wooded edge of the Tabular Hills with the moors climbing away to the north. The interesting church retains its 900 year old crypt (see walk 10). Gallows Hill stands to the south of Lastingham. The gallows for the Manor of Spaunton were set beneath the scarp and all gallows were usually beside a road to act as a warning to other wrongdoers.

The walk passes through the village of Spaunton which has declined since medieval times. Then the Manor of Spaunton covered the area between the River Dove in Farndale and the River Seven in Rosedale. The Manor Farm in Spaunton stands on the site of the 13th century buildings with a Stone Age settlement below that. The Manor Court continues to this day. Woodman Cottage in the village is a cruck house with three bays, it carries a date of 1695 but this indicates the date of rebuilding.

Start:
FROM the road junction near the church walk along the road to Cropton. As you cross the bridge you pass St. Cedd's Well on your left. Turn right then left along the road and on the outskirts of the village pass through a gate straight in front signposted 'public footpath'. Follow the line of trees on your right to a stile. Keep to the edge of the field to a stile and continue over a footbridge. Bear left along the path to another stile and continue over the field. Pass through a gate and follow the edge of the field keeping Hagg Wood on your right. At the end cross a stile beside a gate and turn right up the road. Beware of traffic.

Near the end of the wood turn right on a signposted footpath through a gate which leads into the wood. Take the track on your left which skirts the wood's edge eventually descending to turn left through a gate. Continue along the top side of the woodland until you reach a waymarked path to the left. Cross the field keeping the hedge on your right. Turn right at the end of the field, then turn left through a gateway. Keep the fence on your right to a gate then bear right diagonally over the field passing Oldfield Pond to reach the road. Turn right to the junction.

If you want a short walk the first turn right at the junction is a path that descends into Lastingham. This was the old road and

35

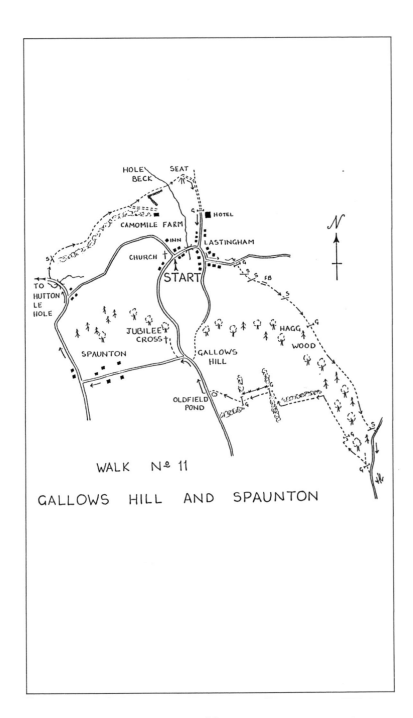

HOLE BECK
SEAT
HOTEL
CAMOMILE FARM
INN
LASTINGHAM
CHURCH
START
FB
TO HUTTON LE HOLE
JUBILEE CROSS
HAGG WOOD
SPAUNTON
GALLOWS HILL
OLDFIELD POND

N

WALK   N° 11

GALLOWS   HILL   AND   SPAUNTON

Gallows Hill is on your right.

The longer walk bears left at the junction and in ten yards turn right alongside the hedge to Jubilee Cross. Here there is an excellent view with Lastingham village below and the moors beyond. Retrace your steps to the road and turn right through the village of Spaunton. At the end of the village turn right down the road to the junction set on unfenced roads.

Bear left and cross over the bridge, after 50 yards turn right at a public footpath sign. Cross over a stile and follow the track to the right on the moorland side of the fields. When the field edge leads to Camomile Farm bear left to a field corner and continue. The path descends steeply to Hole Beck. Cross on stepping stones and climb to a seat offering an excellent view to the west. Continue bearing right to a gate. A road then descends into Lastingham where you turn right back to your starting point.

Hollins Mine, Rosedale

Parking: (SE724959) Rosedale Abbey car park, below the Milburn Arms Hotel.

THIS walk passes through some interesting countryside with excellent views for most of the route. You visit Hollins Mine which was the first of three iron mines where ore was extracted in the valley; it opened in 1856 and by 1861 the ore was taken up a half mile long, rope-hauled tramway to a North Eastern Railway branch line. The ore was carried over the moors to Cleveland for shipment to the iron foundries. The mine closed in 1885 after over 1½ million tons of ironstone had been taken out of the hillside.

Near the White Horse Farm Hotel the walk crosses the road at the foot of Rosedale Chimney Bank. This is one of the steepest road climbs in Britain at 1 in 3. In the 1920's it was used for both motor cycle and car hill climbs and on long distance endurance rallies. The steepest gradient was then 1 in 2½.

Start:
From the crossroads in the centre of the village walk up the road to Egton, passing the entrance to the Milburn Arms Hotel. Beware of traffic as you continue up the road for 700 yards. Turn right opposite the entrance to Heygate Farm on a signposted footpath which crosses a ladder stile over a stone wall. There is an excellent view of central Rosedale at this point including the steep Rosedale Chimney Bank climbing the hillside opposite.

Continue straight ahead down the field to a stile. Cross the next field with the hedge on your right, cross a culverted stream at a bridge and turn right beside the wire fence to the farm. Turn left, then right through a gate following the road between the farm buildings. At the end of the buildings when the road turns right fork left past a pond to a metal gate. Turn right past a barn on your right and continue keeping the stone wall on your right. In the third field turn right over a ladder stile and turn left to a field corner stile with a signpost. At this point you can look across the dale to Hollins Mine and the site of the tramway climbing the hillside to the start of the railway on the moor top where buildings remain.

Turn right at the signpost and keep the stone wall on your right as you descend to a gate onto the road. Turn left along the road to Yatts Farm where you turn right on the signposted bridleway in

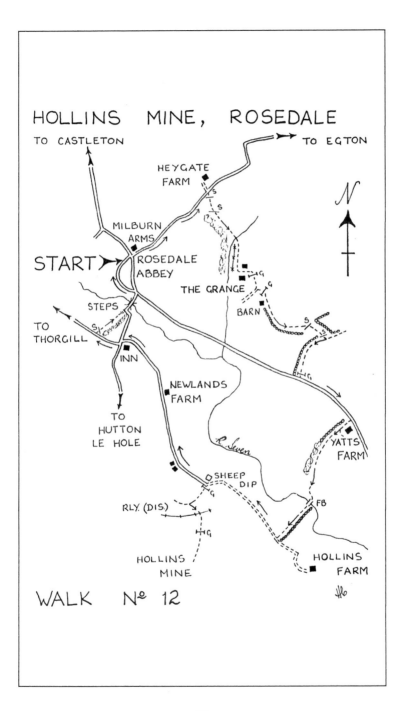

HOLLINS MINE, ROSEDALE

TO CASTLETON

TO EGTON

HEYGATE FARM

MILBURN ARMS

START

ROSEDALE ABBEY

THE GRANGE

BARN

STEPS

TO THORGILL

INN

NEWLANDS FARM

TO HUTTON LE HOLE

R. Seven

YATTS FARM

SHEEP DIP

RLY. (DIS)

FB

HOLLINS MINE

HOLLINS FARM

N

WALK Nº 12

front of the buildings. Fork right, away from the farm buildings, keeping the wall on your right. Continue, eventually descending to a footbridge over the River Seven. Keep the broken down wall on your left as you climb to a stile with Hollins Mine above to your right.

Turn right along the broad track and enjoy the splendid views back across the dale. Cross a cattle grid and continue along the track. Turn left through a gate opposite the sheep dip set within a walled enclosure. Follow the distinct track winding up the hillside and turn left at the fork to a gate. Beyond the gate you cross the bed of the tramway which was used to haul the iron ore to the railway on the moor top. Continue on the track opposite into the vast quarry of Hollins Mine.

Return back down the hillside to the broad track by the sheep dip and turn left. Eventually pass through the car park of the White House Farm Hotel to reach the road near the foot of Rosedale Chimney Bank. Take the road opposite signposted to Thorgill. Turn right over a stile opposite the Red House golf course on the signposted footpath. Descend, keeping the hedge on your right to a set of steps beside a house these lead to the road. Continue over the bridge to the road junction. Turn left along the road into the village centre.

Hamer Moor

Parking: (SE744995) From Rosedale Abbey drive up the Egton road for 3 miles. There is parking on the moor where the Lyke Wake Walk crosses the road.

THIS is a fine moorland walk, especially when the heather is in bloom in August and September. The walk starts close to the site of the former Lettered Board public house at Hamer, you can still see the remains of the building. Joseph Ford was born at the inn in 1870, he grew up to be a local stone mason but he is now remembered for his local history book 'Some Reminiscences and Folk Lore of Danby Parish and District'. Behind the inn are several coal pits; moorland coal was poor quality but it was cheap. The coming of the railways brought better quality coal into the district and the moorland coal pits declined.

Two men died in mysterious circumstances at the inn just over 100 years ago. They were passing travellers and were given a newly plastered room for the night. The following morning they were both discovered dead. After an investigation it was decided that they had either suffocated or they had inhaled fumes from the plaster during the night.

Start:
FROM the car park turn left down the road towards Rosedale Abbey. After 300 yards you pass a public bridleway sign on your left, this is the way you will return. On your right are the ruins of the inn at Hamer. Walk down the unfenced moorland road for 1¼ miles. In August and September when the purple heather is in bloom the moor is a glorious sight. Cross over Hamer Beck and climb out the other side. Turn left at the public bridleway sign along the track over the moors. Keep the stone wall on your left which is the limit of the fields. There are fine moorland views all around.

The track leads to a gate; pass through and turn left towards Low Hamer buildings, then turn right on a broad grassy track which leads to a gateway. Cross diagonally over the next field towards Hamer Beck, cross a sidestream to a gate and continue on the broad track to the road. Turn left at the public bridleway sign over Hamer Beck and pass through the gate.

Walk up to Higher Row Mires Farm, turn right behind the farmhouse for ten yards, then turn left at the end of the buildings through three gates. The fourth gate carries a benchmark carved on the left hand stone post. These arrows with a line above indicate

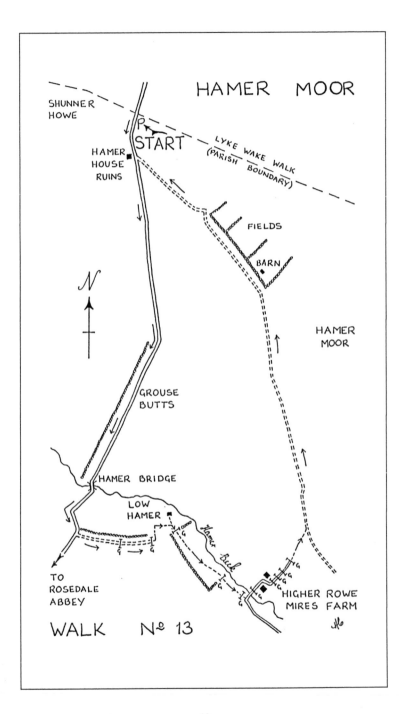

HAMER MOOR

SHUNNER HOWE

P
START

LYKE WAKE WALK
(PARISH BOUNDARY)

HAMER
HOUSE
RUINS

FIELDS

BARN

HAMER
MOOR

N

GROUSE
BUTTS

HAMER BRIDGE

LOW
HAMER

Hamer Beck

TO
ROSEDALE
ABBEY

HIGHER ROWE
MIRES FARM

WALK   N⁰ 13

a known height which can be used for local surveying purposes.

When you pass through the fifth gate above the farm you come back onto Hamer Moor. In front of you is a hollow way which has been carved into the moor by the passage of vehicles wearing away the surface. For a couple of hundred yards the path is indistinct but then a broad path appears on the right. Eventually you see a barn on the skyline with a number of fields surrounded by stone walls. Pass to the left of these enclosures and continue along the distinct track over the moor to rejoin the road near the ruined inn at Hamer. The distinctive mound on the skyline is Shunner Howe, a Bronze Age burial mound. When you reach the road turn right back to the car park.

The Hidden Dale

Parking: (SE724959) Rosedale Abbey car park, below the Milburn Arms Hotel.

ROSEDALE boomed in the middle of the 19th century when iron was discovered in a number of places in the valley. Apart from the three iron mines which operated in the valley there were calcining kilns for burning off waste material and a railway with two spurs to the mines. Beds for workers were at a premium, as someone left a bed to go to work it would be filled by someone else returning from their shift. The industry ceased in the 1920's and the valley has now returned to peace and nature has hidden the mining scars (see walks 12 & 15).

Tucked away off the valley of Rosedale is Northdale formed by Northdale Beck. As no roads pass up the valley you can imagine that anyone living in the few farms on the valley sides may have been unaware of all that had happened in the last century. The walk follows the tree fringed beck upstream to a small footbridge where a climb leads out of the valley for a return beside the River Seven back to Rosedale Abbey.

Start:
FROM the green in the centre of the village walk up the road to Egton passing the entrance to the Milburn Arms Hotel. After 100 yards turn left at the public footpath sign. Cross the car park, pass through a gate and cross over the sports field. In front of you is the tree topped knoll of Hill Plantation. Cross over the stile beside the gate and continue ahead up Northdale. A series of stiles lead up the valley with Northdale Beck on your left. After ¾ of a mile the path crosses Northdale Beck at a stone footbridge in a small wood.

At a signpost ten yards beyond the footbridge turn left uphill with a stone wall on your right. The path continues to rise bearing left between wire fences to reach a farm road near a pond. Turn left along the farm road passing through a gate to reach the Rosedale Abbey-to-Castleton road. At Bell End turn left for 50 yards, then turn right at the bend through a metal gate. A public footpath sign indicates the path which gradually descends with the hedge and wall on your left to a stile.

The path continues with a fence on your left and a stream below on your right. Eventually the path descends a few steps to the left and continues down to the River Seven near a footbridge. Don't cross the footbridge but continue straight ahead to a stile and a path which climbs across a field, firstly with a hedge on the left and later on the right. Continue with the fence on your right into a caravan site. Just beyond the kissing gate is Waterhouse Well, a stone covered water supply. Continue on the stoned road through the caravan site until you pass a children's playground, then turn left to a kissing gate that leads into Rosedale Abbey. Cross over the road and take a path past the few remains of Rosedale's Abbey on your left. Pass through two gates in front of the church and walk back into the centre of Rosedale Abbey.

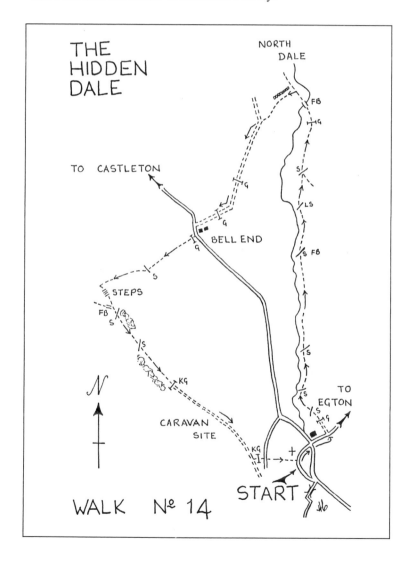

THE HIDDEN DALE

NORTH DALE

TO CASTLETON

BELL END

STEPS

CARAVAN SITE

TO EGTON

START

WALK № 14

The Rosedale Railway

Parking: (SE683989) Take the Castleton road north out of Hutton le Hole for six miles. There is a car park opposite the road junction to Farndale and before the Lion Inn.

WHEN iron ore was discovered in Rosedale in 1856 one of the biggest problems was taking the ore out of the dale to the nearest railway at Pickering. The roads were bad and sometimes impassable for large wagons. By 1861 the North Eastern Railway had built a line over the moors from Battersby Junction. This offered a shorter journey to the ironworks in Cleveland and Durham. In Rosedale two separate branch lines stretched along the western side of the dale to Sheriffs Pit and Hollins Mine, while on the eastern side of the dale the line ran to Rosedale East mines. This walk uses the branch to Rosedale East to return around the head of the dale to Blakey Junction, where at one time there were railwaymen's houses. It was a hard life living 1200 feet up on the moors, especially in winter. In 1929 the line was closed. It is not a right of way but the owner allows walkers to use the track.

Start:
FROM the bottom of the car park walk ten yards down the road and turn left along the track signposted 'Footpath to Rosedale'. Walk along the right hand side of the cutting. This was where the mineral railway passed under the road, the only bridge on the 19 mile railway. Cross over the railway bed and continue on a track that begins to descend into the valley. At this point you can see across the valley to the right some of the large calcining kilns where waste material was burnt off. You can also follow the line of the railway from Rosedale East Mines along the hillside to circle the head of the dale to Blakey Junction where it joined the track you have just crossed from Hollins Mine and Sheriffs Pit.

The track descends into the valley and you can see ahead the three farms in the valley bottom through which you will pass. When you reach a broad rough track turn right and continue down to Moorlands Farm. Pass between the farm buildings and turn left at the end of the farmhouse to a wooden gate. Continue on a broad track with a stone wall on your left to Hollin Bush Farm. Keep the farm buildings on your left and when the track swings left turn right and climb over a stone stile set between two gates (not the one to the left of the gate in front of you). Walk diagonally over the field and pass through a small valley that descends to a

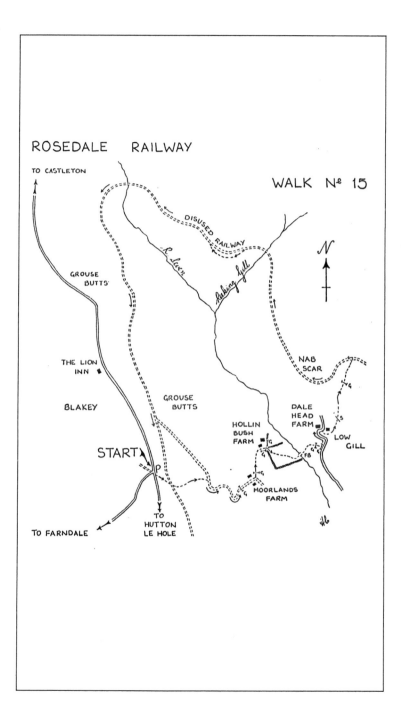

ROSEDALE   RAILWAY

TO CASTLETON

WALK Nº 15

DISUSED RAILWAY

R. Seven

parking field

N

GROUSE
BUTTS

THE LION
INN

BLAKEY

GROUSE
BUTTS

NAB
SCAR

G

S

DALE
HEAD
FARM

LOW
GILL

HOLLIN
BUSH
FARM

G
G

G

FB

START

P

G

G

MOORLANDS
FARM

TO FARNDALE

TO
HUTTON
LE HOLE

footbridge over the tree fringed River Seven.

Cross the field to a gateway below Dale Head Farm and continue over the field to the road. Turn left along the road and then right before the farmhouse on a path signposted 'Bridleway to Great Fryup Dale'. The track sweeps left around a building and climbs with a stream below on your right. Pause as you climb steeply out of the valley, on your right you can see the calcining kilns above the railway track. Keep the wire fence on your right to a gate and continue uphill until you reach the bed of the railway. Turn left along the former railway and enjoy the excellent views down into the dale.

As you skirt Nab Scar you pass a dressed stone siding, it was used to remove building stone from Nab Scar Quarry. The railway continues over the lofty embankment above Reeking Gill and then the path climbs above a waterlogged cutting. Eventually you cross the embankment above the River Seven at the head of the dale. Also you pass a ruined brick structure that used to support a water tank for topping up the engines. In the final mile the railway passes below the Lion Inn to reach Blakey Junction from where you started out. The railway cottages have vanished but you will recognise the cutting to take the line to Battersby Junction.